Copyright © 2025 by Holly Symons
All rights reserved.

No part of this book may be reproduced, scanned, or distributed in any printed or electronic form without permission.
This book is a work of fiction. Names, characters, places, and incidents are either the product of the author's imagination or used fictitiously.
Hardback - ISBN: 978-1-923567-51-1
Paperback - ISBN: 978-1-923567-52-8
eBook - ISBN: 978-1-923567-53-5

Cover design by **Holly Symons**
First Edition

For More, Please Visit
HollySymons.com.au

Dear Reader,

If you have ever opened a message that says, "Could you bring a plate," and felt your brain throw confetti and panic at the same time, this book is for you. I wrote **Bring a Plate** to turn that mini moment of stress into a quick smile and an easy plan.

Inside, you will find bright, reliable sides that travel well, taste great at room temperature, and use supermarket ingredients you can grab on the way. Potatoes for the comfort crowd, big bowl salads for colour and crunch, slaws that hold on a hot day, warm breads that make everything feel generous, pasta salads that stay creamy, dips that go with absolutely everything, and sweet finishes that look like you tried very hard, even when you did not.

Recipes are metric first, spoon-friendly, and written for real life, short steps, clear timing, and make-ahead notes so you can prep early and relax later. I added simple icons for GF friendly, DF options, vegetarian, nut-free, ten-minute hands-on, and Travels Well, so you can choose fast and feel confident about feeding a mix of people.

Use the book in three ways. One, grab a hero recipe and go; the Pink Sunshine Potato Salad or the Roasted Pumpkin and Feta bowl never fails. Two, mix a salad and a dip, that is a complete plate with crackers or flatbreads. Three, build a tiny spread, a salad, a bread, and a sweet, perfect for when you want to look organised without breaking a sweat.

Swap what you need, use herbs you have, and rely on the make-ahead tips. A good bring-a-plate is not fancy; it is generous, colourful, and easy to share. You have got this, and I am cheering for you from the beach at sunrise.

With love and sunshine,

Holly Symons

P.S

Salad Storage and Safety

Keep cold salads chilled under 4 °C. Do not leave mayo-based salads out longer than 2 hours in summer heat.

Bring a Plate

The Ultimate Australian BBQ Sides, Salads

HOLLY SYMONS

Things to do with potatoes

1. Pink Sunshine Coast Lemon-Chive Potato Salad
2. Pub-Style Cheesy Potato Bake
3. Herbed Chat Potatoes with Lemon Myrtle
4. Roast Potato and Green Bean Toss
5. Warm Bacon and Onion Potato Salad
6. Potato, Corn and Chive Salad, creamy dressing

Big bowl salads

7. Roasted Pumpkin and Feta Salad with Maple Balsamic
8. Pear, Rocket and Parmesan with Lemon
9. Cabbage, Apple and Smoked Cheddar Salad
10. Mango, Cucumber and Lime Picnic Salad
11. Charred Corn and Avocado Salad
12. Rice Noodle Crunch Salad with Ginger-Lime

Creamy & Crunchy Slaws

13. Pineapple and Coriander Coleslaw
14. Sesame-Free Asian Crunch Slaw
15. Beetroot and Carrot Rainbow Slaw
16. Smoky BBQ Coleslaw
17. Dill Pickle Coleslaw, No Seeds
18. Red Cabbage and Carrot Lime Slaw

Breads and bakes

19. Cheesy Pull-Apart Party Loaf
20. Herb and Garlic Tear-and-Share Bread
21. Garlic and Herb Flatbreads

22. Soft Dinner Rolls, No-Knead
23. Olive Oil Focaccia Slab, Backyard BBQ

Pasta salads

24. Roasted Capsicum and Olive Pasta Salad
25. Sun-Dried Tomato and Basil Pasta Salad
26. Creamy Avocado Pasta Salad
27. Greek Lemon Orzo Salad

Dips, sauces and vinaigrettes

28. Roasted Capsicum and Feta Whip
29. Avocado Lime Crema
30. Smoky Eggplant Dip
31. Sweet Chilli Yogurt Dipping Sauce

Fruit and sweet finishes

32. Grilled Pineapple Skewers with Coconut Lime Cream
33. Mango Pavlova Cups
34. Lamington Trifle Jars
35. Berry Eton Mess, Down Under

Things to do with potatoes

Pink Sunshine Potato Salad, with Beetroot and Egg

GF, seed-free, DF option, travels well

Serves 10 to 12

You need

- 1.5 kg baby potatoes, scrubbed
- 250 g Greek yogurt, or coconut yogurt
- 4 tbsp mayonnaise
- 3 tbsp lemon juice, plus 1 tsp zest
- 2 tbsp extra virgin olive oil
- 1 small garlic clove, finely grated
- 3 tbsp chives, chopped
- 2 tbsp parsley, chopped
- 1¼ tsp fine salt, ¾ tsp pepper
- 1 tin beetroot chunks, 425 g, drained, reserve 2 tbsp beet liquid
- 6 hard-boiled eggs, peeled and chopped

Do this

1. Boil potatoes in salted water until just tender, 12 to 15 minutes. Drain, cool 10 minutes, halve.
2. For a bright pink stain, drizzle the warm potatoes with 1 to 2 tbsp reserved beet liquid. Toss gently and rest 5 minutes.

3. Whisk yogurt, mayonnaise, lemon juice and zest, olive oil, garlic, salt and pepper.
4. Toss potatoes with dressing until coated.
5. Fold in herbs and chopped eggs.
6. Fold in beetroot chunks so some colour runs through the salad. Chill 30 to 60 minutes. Taste, add a squeeze of lemon and a pinch of salt before serving.

Optional extras

- 50 g crumbled feta for a salty pop
- 2 celery sticks, fine dice, for crunch
- Extra chives on top to finish

2) Pub Style Cheesy Potato Bake

GF, NF

Serves 10

You need

- 1.8 kg potatoes, thin slices
- 1 tbsp butter or olive oil
- 1 large onion, thinly sliced
- 2 garlic cloves, crushed
- 500 ml thickened cream
- 250 ml milk
- 1 tbsp cornflour, GF
- 1 tsp salt, ½ tsp pepper
- 200 g tasty cheese, grated
- 50 g parmesan, grated

Do this

1. Heat oven to 190 °C. Butter a large baking dish.
2. Soften onion in a pan with oil 5 minutes, then add garlic 1 minute.

3. Whisk cornflour into milk, then stir in cream, salt, pepper.
4. Layer half the potatoes, half the onions, half the cheese. Repeat. Pour cream mix over.
5. Cover with foil 40 minutes, uncover 20 to 25 minutes until golden and bubbling. Rest 10 minutes.

Dairy-free swap: Use coconut cream and DF cheese; it still browns nicely.

3) Herbed Chat Potatoes with Lemon Myrtle

GF, DF, seed free

Serves 8

You need

- 1.5 kg chat potatoes
- 2 tbsp olive oil
- 1 tsp ground lemon myrtle
- 1 tsp salt
- ½ tsp pepper
- 2 tbsp dill or parsley, chopped

Do this

1. Heat oven to 210 °C. Toss potatoes with oil, lemon myrtle, salt, and pepper.
2. Roast 30 to 35 minutes until crisp at the edges.
3. Toss with herbs, serve warm.

4) Roast Potato and Green Bean Toss, warm lemon dressing

GF, DF, seed-free

Serves 8

You need

- 1.2 kg potatoes, 3 cm cubes
- 2 tbsp olive oil
- 300 g green beans, trimmed
- 1 small red onion, thinly sliced

Dressing

- 3 tbsp olive oil
- 2 tbsp lemon juice
- 1 tsp honey
- ½ tsp salt, pepper

Do this

1. Roast potatoes at 210 °C with oil and a pinch of salt, 30 minutes.
2. Microwave or steam beans 2 to 3 minutes until just tender.
3. Whisk dressing.
4. Toss hot potatoes with beans, onion and dressing. Serve warm.

5) Warm Bacon and Onion Potato Salad

GF, seed free

Serves 8

You need

- 1.5 kg potatoes, chunks
- 6 rashers bacon, chopped
- 1 large onion, thin slices
- 3 tbsp apple cider vinegar
- 2 tbsp olive oil
- 1 tsp sugar or honey
- 1 tsp salt, ½ tsp pepper
- 2 tbsp parsley, chopped

Do this

1. Boil potatoes until tender, drain.
2. Fry bacon until crisp, remove, leave 2 tbsp fat in pan, add onion, cook 5 minutes.
3. Stir in vinegar, oil, sugar, salt, pepper to make a warm dressing.
4. Toss potatoes with bacon, onion and dressing, finish with parsley.

6) Potato, Corn and Chive Salad, creamy dressing

GF, seed free

Serves 8

You need

- 1.2 kg potatoes, 3 cm cubes
- 2 corn cobs, kernels cut, or 1½ cups frozen corn, thawed
- ¾ cup mayonnaise
- ¼ cup sour cream or Greek yogurt
- 1 tbsp lemon juice
- 1 tsp garlic powder
- 2 tbsp chives, chopped
- 1 tsp salt, ½ tsp pepper

Do this

1. Boil potatoes until tender, drain, and cool for 10 minutes.
2. Pan char the corn in a dry pan for 3 minutes for extra flavour, optional.
3. Mix dressing ingredients, fold in potatoes, corn and chives. Chill 45 minutes.

Big bowl salads

15) Roasted Pumpkin and Feta Salad with Maple Balsamic

GF, NF, V-option

Serves 8 as a side

You need

- 1.2 kg butternut or Kent pumpkin, peeled, 3 cm cubes
- 1 red onion, wedges
- 2 tbsp olive oil, 1 tsp salt, pepper
- 100 g rocket
- 150 g feta, crumbled

Dressing 3 tbsp olive oil, 1½ tbsp balsamic, 1 tbsp maple syrup, 1 tbsp lemon juice, 1 tsp smooth Dijon, pinch salt

Do this

1. Heat oven to 210 C. Toss pumpkin and onion with oil, salt, pepper. Roast 25 to 30 minutes until caramelised. Cool 10 minutes.
2. Whisk dressing.
3. In a big bowl, add rocket, warm veg, dressing, toss gently. Top with feta

16) Pear, Rocket and Parmesan with Lemon

GF, NF

Serves 6 to 8

You need

- 120 g rocket
- 2 ripe pears, thinly sliced
- 60 g Parmesan, shaved
- pine nuts – optional

Dressing: 3 tbsp olive oil, 1½ tbsp lemon juice, 1 tsp honey, pinch salt and pepper

Do this

1. Whisk dressing.
2. Toss rocket and pears with dressing.
3. Finish with Parmesan.

Optional: Add a crisp prosciutto shard if you want a salty crunch.

17) Cabbage, Apple and Smoked Cheddar Salad

GF, NF

Serves 8

You need

- 600 g green cabbage, finely shredded
- 2 large apples, matchsticks, toss in 1 tsp lemon juice
- 2 carrots, grated
- 120 g smoked cheddar, small cubes
- 3 spring onions, thin slices

Dressing ½ cup (125 ml) mayonnaise, 2 tbsp apple cider vinegar, 2 tsp honey, 1 tsp smooth Dijon, ½ tsp salt, pepper

Do this

1. Whisk dressing until smooth.
2. Toss cabbage, apple, carrot and spring onion with dressing.
3. Fold in cheddar. Chill 20 to 30 minutes.

18) Mango, Cucumber and Lime Picnic Salad

GF, DF, NF, V

Serves 6 to 8

You need

- 2 ripe mangoes, 2 cm cubes
- 2 Lebanese cucumbers, seeds scraped, half moons
- ¼ small red onion, very thin slices
- ¼ cup coriander leaves, chopped, optional

Dressing 2 tbsp olive oil, 3 tbsp lime juice, 1 tsp honey, pinch salt

Do this

1. Whisk dressing.
2. Toss mango, cucumber and onion.
3. Add dressing and coriander. Chill 15 minutes.

Optional Add 1 avocado, cubes, just before serving.

19) Charred Corn and Avocado Salad

GF, DF, NF, V

Serves 8

You need

- 4 corn cobs, husks off
- 2 tbsp olive oil, divided
- 1 red capsicum, small dice
- 3 spring onions, thinly sliced
- 2 avocados, cubes
- ¼ cup chopped coriander or parsley

Dressing 3 tbsp lime juice, 2 tbsp olive oil, ½ tsp salt, pepper

Do this

1. Brush corn with a little oil. Char on BBQ or grill pan, 8 to 10 minutes, turning. Cool, cut kernels off.
2. Whisk dressing.
3. Toss warm corn with capsicum and spring onion. Fold in avocado and herbs. Dress and serve.

20) Rice Noodle Crunch Salad with Ginger Lime

GF, DF, NF, V

Serves 8

You need

- 200 g rice vermicelli or thin rice sticks
- 400 g crunchy slaw mix, or 300 g cabbage plus 2 carrots, shredded
- 1 red capsicum, thin strips
- 1 Lebanese cucumber, seeds scraped, thin batons
- 1 cup snow peas, thin slices
- ½ cup mint and coriander leaves, chopped

   Dressing 4 tbsp lime juice, 2 tbsp tamari, 1 tbsp brown sugar or maple, 1 tbsp grated ginger, 1 small garlic clove, 2 tbsp olive oil

Do this

1. Soak noodles in hot water until just tender. Drain very well, snip a few times with scissors.
2. Whisk dressing.
3. Toss noodles with veg and herbs. Add dressing, mix until glossy.

Creamy & Crunchy Slaws

21) Pineapple and Coriander Coleslaw

GF, NF, DF option, travels well

Serves 8

You need

- 600 g green cabbage, finely shredded
- 2 large carrots, grated
- 4 spring onions, thin slices
- 300 g pineapple, small cubes, well drained
- ¼ cup coriander leaves, chopped

Dressing ¾ cup (180 g) mayonnaise, 2 tbsp lime juice, 1 tbsp honey or maple, 1 tsp smooth Dijon, ½ tsp salt, pepper

Do this

1. Whisk dressing until glossy.
2. Toss cabbage, carrot and spring onion. Fold in pineapple and coriander.
3. Chill 20 to 30 minutes to soften slightly.

   DF use vegan mayo.

22) Sesame-Free Asian Crunch Slaw

GF, DF, NF, travels well

Serves 8

You need

- 500 g wombok, finely shredded
- 200 g red cabbage, finely shredded
- 2 carrots, matchsticks
- 1 red capsicum, thin strips
- 1 cup snow peas, thin slices
- ¼ cup mint and coriander, chopped

Dressing 3 tbsp lime juice, 2 tbsp rice vinegar, 2 tbsp tamari, 1 tbsp maple, 1 tbsp grated ginger, 1 small garlic clove, 2 tbsp neutral oil, ½ tsp salt

Do this

1. Whisk dressing.
2. Toss slaw and herbs with dressing until shiny.
3. Serve fresh and crunchy.

    Optional: Sprinkle GF crispy shallots at the table.

23) Beetroot and Carrot Rainbow Slaw

GF, NF, travels well

Serves 8

You need

- 300 g raw beetroot, peeled, coarsely grated
- 300 g carrots, coarsely grated
- 250 g red cabbage, finely shredded
- 1 small green apple, matchsticks
- 2 tbsp parsley or dill, chopped

Dressing: ½ cup (120 g) Greek yogurt or coconut yogurt, ¼ cup mayonnaise, 1 tbsp lemon juice, 1 tsp honey, 1 tsp smooth Dijon, ½ tsp salt, pepper

Do this

1. Whisk dressing.
2. Toss the veggies and apple, then fold through the dressing.
3. Chill for 30 minutes so the colours mingle and the veg softens.

24) Smoky BBQ Coleslaw

GF, NF, travels well

Serves 10

You need

- 600 g green cabbage, shredded
- 200 g red cabbage, shredded
- 2 large carrots, grated
- ½ small red onion, very thin slices

Dressing ½ cup (120 g) mayonnaise, ¼ cup sour cream or Greek yogurt, 2 tbsp apple cider vinegar, 2 tbsp BBQ sauce, ½ tsp smoked paprika, ½ tsp garlic powder, ¾ tsp salt, pepper

Do this

1. Whisk dressing smooth.
2. Toss slaw mix with dressing.
3. Chill 20 minutes. Taste and salt again if needed.

25) Dill Pickle Coleslaw, No Seeds

GF, NF, travels well

Serves 8

You need

- 600 g green cabbage, finely shredded
- 2 carrots, grated
- 3 spring onions, thinly sliced
- ¾ cup chopped dill pickles

Dressing: ½ cup (120 g) mayonnaise, 2 tbsp pickle brine, 1 tsp smooth Dijon, 1 tsp honey, ½ tsp garlic powder, ½ tsp salt, pepper, 1 tbsp chopped fresh dill

Do this

1. Whisk dressing.
2. Toss cabbage, carrot and spring onion. Fold in pickles and dill with dressing.
3. Chill 30 minutes. Add a splash more brine if you like it sharper.

26) Red Cabbage and Carrot Lime Slaw

GF, DF, NF, travels well

Serves 8

You need

- 500 g red cabbage, finely shredded
- 300 g carrots, matchsticks
- ¼ small red onion, very thin slices
- ¼ cup coriander or mint, chopped

Dressing 3 tbsp lime juice, 3 tbsp olive oil, 1 tsp honey, ½ tsp salt, pepper

Do this

1. Whisk dressing.
2. Toss slaw and herbs with dressing until lightly coated.

Breads and bakes

39) Cheesy Pull-Apart Party Loaf

Travels Well, NF, GF option

Serves 10 to 12

You need

- 1 large crusty cob loaf, about 800 g
- 120 g butter, melted
- 2 garlic cloves, finely grated
- 2 tbsp parsley, chopped
- 250 g grated tasty cheese
- 150 g grated mozzarella
- ½ tsp salt, pinch pepper

Do this

1. Heat oven to 180 C. Place loaf on a sheet of foil on a tray.
2. Cut a grid of deep slits across the top, 2 cm apart, do not cut through.
3. Mix butter, garlic, parsley, salt, pepper. Spoon into the cuts.

4. Push cheeses into the cuts. Wrap loosely in foil.
5. Bake for 15 minutes, then unwrap and bake for an additional 10 to 12 minutes, or until melted and golden.

GF friendly. Use a gluten-free cob loaf, or pack 10 to 12 small GF dinner rolls tightly into a lined tin, then follow the same butter and cheese method.

40) Herb and Garlic Tear-and-Share Bread

Quick no-yeast dough, NF, GF option

Serves 10

You need

- 500 g self-rising flour
- 500 g Greek yogurt
- 1 tsp fine salt
- 60 g butter, melted
- 2 garlic cloves, finely grated
- 2 tbsp mixed herbs, chopped, parsley, chives, oregano

Do this

1. Heat oven to 200 °C. Line a 23 cm cake tin.
2. Stir flour, yogurt, and salt to a soft dough. Lightly flour hands.
3. Divide into 12 balls, arrange snugly in the tin.
4. Mix butter, garlic, and herbs. Brush half of the dough.

5. Bake 20 to 25 minutes until risen and lightly golden. Brush with remaining butter and serve warm.

   GF friendly Use gluten-free self-rising flour. If your blend has no xanthan gum, add 1 tsp for better structure.

41) Garlic and Herb Flatbreads

Pan-cooked, V, DF option, GF option

Makes 8

You need

- 300 g self-raising flour, plus extra for dusting
- 300 g Greek yogurt, or coconut yogurt
- 1 tsp fine salt
- 1 tsp garlic powder
- 2 tbsp olive oil, for cooking
- Optional finish, 30 g melted butter with 1 grated garlic clove and 1 tbsp chopped parsley

Do this

1. Mix flour, yogurt, salt, and garlic powder to a soft dough. Rest 5 minutes.
2. Divide into 8 pieces. Roll the dough between baking paper sheets to a thickness of 3 to 4 mm.

3. Heat a non-stick pan with a thin film of oil. Cook each flatbread 1 to 2 minutes per side until puffed and spotted.
4. Brush with the optional garlic butter and serve.

GF friendly Use GF self-raising flour. Roll the dough between baking paper sheets and cook gently to prevent cracking.

42) Soft Dinner Rolls, No-Knead

Fluffy tray rolls, NF, GF option

Makes 12

You need

- 500 g bread flour
- 7 g instant yeast
- 40 g sugar
- 10 g fine salt
- 300 ml warm milk, or warm water for DF
- 60 g melted butter, or 50 ml neutral oil for DF
- 1 large egg, optional for richer rolls

Do this

1. In a bowl whisk milk, melted butter, yeast, sugar, egg if using. Add flour and salt, mix with a spoon until no dry spots remain. Dough will be sticky.
2. Cover and rise in a warm spot 60 to 90 minutes until doubled, or chill overnight.

3. Oil hands, divide into 12 balls. Arrange in a lined 23 x 33 cm tin. Cover and rise 30 to 45 minutes.
4. Bake at 190 °C for 18 to 22 minutes until golden. Brush warm tops with a little melted butter.

Make ahead. Cool, freeze in a bag, rewarm wrapped in foil.

GF note. The easiest path is to use a GF bread mix, following the packet's liquid instructions, and then shape the mixture into rolls in a muffin tin for added support.

43) Olive Oil Focaccia Slab, Backyard BBQ

Crispy edges, soft middle, GF option, V, NF

Serves 12

You need

- 500 g strong flour
- 7 g instant yeast
- 10 g fine salt
- 400 ml warm water
- 50 ml extra virgin olive oil, plus extra for the pan and the top
- 1 tsp flaky salt
- 1 tbsp rosemary leaves

Do this

1. In a large bowl mix flour, yeast, salt, water, and olive oil to a loose batter-like dough. Cover, rest 10 minutes, then give 30 seconds of folds with a spatula. Repeat rest and folds twice more.

2. Oil a 23 x 33 cm tin. Pour in the dough, knead it with your hands, and stretch it to the corners. Cover and rise 45 to 60 minutes until bubbly.
3. Heat oven to 220 C. Oil fingertips dimple the surface deeply. Drizzle 1 to 2 tbsp olive oil, sprinkle rosemary and flaky salt.
4. Bake 22 to 28 minutes until deeply golden. Rest 10 minutes, then lift out and slice.

Make ahead, best the day it is baked. Re-crisp slices on the BBQ plate or in a 200 °C oven for 5 minutes.

GF note: Use a gluten-free focaccia mix, spread into the oiled pan and follow the same topping and bake.

Pasta salads

47) Roasted Capsicum and Olive Pasta Salad

GF option, DF, NF, travels well

Serves 8

You need

- 500 g short pasta, GF if needed
- 2 roasted red capsicums, strips, well drained
- 1 small red onion, very thin slices
- 150 g pitted kalamata olives, halved
- ¼ cup parsley, chopped

Dressing 4 tbsp olive oil, 2 tbsp red wine vinegar, 1 tsp smooth Dijon, ½ tsp dried oregano, ¾ tsp salt, pepper

Do this

1. Cook pasta in salted water until just tender. Rinse under cold water, drain very well.
2. Whisk dressing.
3. Toss pasta with capsicum, onion, olives, parsley and dressing. Chill for 1 hour.

   Make ahead Up to 24 hours. Add a splash of oil and a pinch of salt before serving.

48) Sun-Dried Tomato and Basil Pasta Salad

GF option, seed aware, NF, travels well

Serves 8

You need

- 500 g spiral pasta, GF if needed
- 150 g soft semi-dried tomatoes, strips, choose low-seed pieces
- 1 cup roasted capsicum strips, optional for extra colour
- 1 cup baby bocconcini, halved, or diced feta
- ½ cup basil leaves, torn

Dressing 3 tbsp olive oil, 2 tbsp tomato oil from the jar, 1 tbsp balsamic, 1 tsp smooth Dijon, ½ tsp salt, pepper

Do this

1. Cook pasta, rinse cold, drain very well.
2. Whisk dressing.

3. Toss pasta with tomatoes, capsicum, cheese and basil. Dress and chill for 30 to 60 minutes.

   Seed aware: If seeds are a concern, use roasted capsicum only and skip tomatoes, or use a seed-free red pesto instead.

49) Creamy Avocado Pasta Salad

GF option, DF option, NF, travels well

Serves 8

You need

- 500 g shell or spiral pasta, GF if needed
- 2 ripe avocados, cubes
- 1 cup corn kernels, thawed
- 3 spring onions, thin slices
- ¼ cup coriander or parsley, chopped

Dressing ¾ cup Greek yogurt or coconut yogurt, 2 tbsp mayonnaise, 3 tbsp lime juice, 1 small garlic clove microplaned, ¾ tsp salt, pepper

Do this

1. Cook pasta, rinse cold, drain very well.
2. Whisk dressing until smooth.
3. Toss pasta with corn and spring onion. Fold in avocado and herbs gently.

    Make ahead: Keep avocado and a little extra lime aside. Fold in just before serving so it stays green.

50) Greek Lemon Orzo Salad

GF option, DF, NF, seed aware, travels well

Serves 8

You need

- 400 g orzo, or GF version
- 1 Lebanese cucumber, seeds scraped, small dice
- 250 g cherry tomatoes, halved, choose low seed varieties or omit if needed
- ½ small red onion, very thin slices
- 150 g feta, small cubes, optional
- ¼ cup dill and parsley, chopped

Dressing 4 tbsp olive oil, 3 tbsp lemon juice, 1 tsp lemon zest, ½ tsp oregano, ¾ tsp salt, pepper

Do this

1. Cook orzo until just tender. Rinse cold, drain very well.
2. Whisk dressing.
3. Toss orzo with cucumber, tomatoes, onion, herbs and dressing. Fold in feta if using.

   Make ahead Up to 24 hours. Add a squeeze of lemon and a pinch of salt before serving

Dips, sauces and vinaigrettes

51) Roasted Capsicum and Feta Whip

GF, NF

Makes about 2 cups

You need

- 2 large roasted red capsicums, drained very well
- 200 g Danish feta
- 150 g Greek yogurt, or coconut yogurt
- 1 tbsp lemon juice
- 1 tbsp olive oil
- Pinch chilli flakes, optional
- Salt, only if needed

Do this

Blend everything until silky. Chill 30 minutes to thicken.

Serve with veg sticks, crackers, and flatbreads.

52) Avocado Lime Crema

GF, NF, DF option

Makes about 2 cups

You need

- 2 ripe avocados
- 150 g Greek yogurt, or coconut yogurt
- 3 tbsp lime juice
- 1 small garlic clove, microplaned
- ½ tsp salt, pepper
- 2 tbsp water to loosen, if needed
- 2 tbsp chopped coriander or parsley, optional

Do this

Blend until very smooth. Thin with water to drizzling consistency.

Serve with grilled prawns, fish, tacos, corn, veg skewers

53) Smoky Eggplant Dip

GF, NF, sesame free

Makes about 2 cups

You need

- 2 large eggplants
- 2 tbsp lemon juice
- 2 tbsp olive oil
- 1 small garlic clove, microplaned
- ½ tsp smoked paprika
- ¾ tsp salt, pepper
- 2 tbsp chopped parsley

Do this

1. Char whole eggplants on the BBQ or roast at 220 °C until collapsed and very soft, 30 to 40 minutes. Cool, peel, and drain in a sieve for 10 minutes.
2. Mash flesh with lemon, oil, garlic, paprika, salt, and pepper. Fold in parsley.

54) Sweet Chilli Yogurt Dipping Sauce

GF, NF, DF option

Makes about 1½ cups

You need

- 250 g Greek yogurt, or coconut yogurt
- 3 tbsp sweet chilli sauce, GF
- 1 tbsp lime juice
- ½ tsp garlic powder
- Pinch salt

Do this

Whisk smooth.

Serve with grilled chicken, prawns, veg fritters, and potato wedges.

Fruit and sweet finishes

65) Grilled Pineapple Skewers with Coconut Lime Cream

GF, DF, NF

Serves 6

You need

- 1 ripe pineapple, peeled, cored, cut into spears
- 1 tbsp brown sugar, optional
- 1 tsp ground cinnamon, optional
- Metal or soaked wooden skewers

Coconut lime cream

- 400 ml can coconut cream, chilled overnight
- 1½ tbsp icing sugar
- 1 tsp lime zest, plus lime wedges to serve

Do this

1. Scoop the thick coconut cream into a bowl, beat with icing sugar and lime zest to soft peaks. Chill.
2. Toss pineapple with brown sugar and cinnamon if using. Thread onto skewers.
3. Grill on a hot BBQ, 2 to 3 minutes per side, until char lines appear.
4. Serve warm with coconut cream and lime wedges.

Make ahead. Whip the cream up to 24 hours ahead, keep very cold.

66) Mango Pavlova Cups

GF, DF option

Serves 12 mini cups

You need

- 12 store-bought mini meringue nests, GF
- 300 ml thickened cream, or coconut cream for DF
- 1 tbsp icing sugar
- 1 tsp vanilla
- 2 ripe mangoes, small cubes

Seed-free mango coulis

- 1 ripe mango, flesh only
- 1 tbsp lime juice
- 1 tsp honey

Do this

1. Beat cream with icing sugar and vanilla to soft peaks.

2. Blend the coulis ingredients until smooth.
3. Fill nests with cream, top with mango cubes, and drizzle coulis.

Make ahead. Assemble within 1 hour of serving so nests stay crisp. Keep cream and fruit prepped in separate bowls.

67) Lamington Trifle Jars

GF option, NF

Makes 8 x 250 ml jars

You need

- 500 g sponge or lamington fingers, GF if needed, cut in cubes
- ½ cup seedless strawberry jam, loosen with 2 tbsp hot water
- 600 ml ready custard, dairy or coconut custard
- 300 ml thickened cream, whipped, or coconut cream
- 80 g desiccated coconut, lightly toasted
- 80 ml chocolate sauce, store-bought or homemade

Do this

1. Swirl jam through the sponge cubes.
2. Layer in jars, sponge, custard, chocolate sauce, whipped cream, and coconut. Repeat to fill.
3. Finish with a drizzle of chocolate and a sprinkle of coconut.

68) Berry Eton Mess, Down Under

GF, seed aware

Serves 8

You need

- 400 g blueberries and strawberries, chopped small
- 2 tbsp sugar
- 1 tsp lemon zest
- 300 ml thickened cream, or coconut cream for DF
- 1 tbsp icing sugar
- 1 tsp vanilla
- 6 store-bought meringue nests, roughly crushed

Seed-free berry sauce

- 250 g raspberries or mixed berries, simmer with 2 tbsp water and 1 tbsp sugar for 3 to 4 minutes, press through a sieve to remove seeds, cool

Do this

1. Toss blueberries and strawberries with sugar and lemon zest. Rest 10 minutes.
2. Whip cream with icing sugar and vanilla to soft peaks.
3. Fold the fruit and crushed meringue through the cream in big ribbons.
4. Spoon into bowls and drizzle the seed-free berry sauce.

Make ahead. Keep components separate. Fold together right before serving so it stays cloud-light.

www.ingramcontent.com/pod-product-compliance
Lightning Source LLC
Chambersburg PA
CBHW041219070526
44584CB00001B/10